INSPIRING STORIES FOR AMAZING BOYS

Empowering Tales of Courage,
Confidence, and Kindness

Katie Wensley

Contents

Introduction

Psst... Want to know a secret?

There's something super cool inside this book: it's all about YOU!

Inspiring Stories for Amazing Boys is packed with ten awesome adventures, showing how boys just like you can be brave even when they're scared, kind even when they feel jealous, and do the right thing even when it's hard. From video game battles to tough days at school, these boys always find ways to keep going—and you will too!

You're already amazing just as you are! Life can get tricky sometimes, but you're much stronger than you think. By the time you finish this book, you'll feel ready to take on anything that comes your way!

Happy reading!

The Not-So-Superhero

"**N**oah! You're going to hurt yourself, buddy," eight-year-old Noah's mother called, worried her son might fall and bump his head. Noah didn't listen; he continued to race around the house.

"Look, mommy! Look! I'm the fastest boy in the world," he shouted while giggling and doing his very best to make his little legs go even faster. Skillfully, he avoided running into any furniture.

Noah was an intelligent boy with a big dream. He wanted to be a superhero, just like Superman, Batman, or one of the Avengers. After school, he never missed watching movies about superheroes and adored how people marveled at them. They were strong and brave—everything Noah wanted to be.

"Mom," he suddenly called, stopping himself by grabbing onto his mother's leg and trying to swipe a piece of fried chicken from a plate she was carrying. His mother chuckled and raised the plate out of his reach.

"Yes, darling?" she asked while passing him plates to set the dinner table.

"Mom, do you think if I practice enough, I might become like Superman too?" Noah asked curiously with a tilt of his head. Noah arranged the plates at the table while awaiting his mother's answer.

His mother stood with her hand stroking her chin and eyes pointed at the ceiling. She was thinking long and hard. Noah was growing excited to hear what she would say. He could hardly stand still, arms fidgeting away, and legs pacing about.

"I think you can," his mother finally confirmed with a nod of her head. She looked so sure of it that Noah became extremely happy. He cheered, spending the rest of the day running around to get faster and lifting his dad's gym bag to get stronger.

He ran to the mirror every so often and checked to see if he had grown muscles. Lifting his shirt, a frown formed on his lips as he saw no abs yet.

"Dad, do I look more muscle-y to you?" he asked hoping his father would see some difference in his physique.

His father looked over, eyes widening. He lifted the boy's arms and wiggled them around before lightly tapping the top of his head.

"You know what? I think you do, buddy!" he said. Noah cheered in excitement.

"Yes, yes, yes! I'm going to be a superhero soon, you know, dad? Like Superman! Or maybe even the Hulk." Noah's eyes lit up as he daydreamed about being a superhero, his imagination running wild.

His father, with a gentle smile and a stretch, let out a big yawn. "Being strong and fast is cool, but they aren't the only things that make you a superhero, buddy," he said, his voice calm and wise.

"Huh? What do you mean? All superheroes are super strong and super fast. Some of them fly too, but Mommy says I can't do that, and she doesn't want me trying either," Noah said with a pout, remembering the earlier conversation. His father chuckled, gently ruffling Noah's hair—something Noah never enjoyed. He sulked even more.

"You'll see, kiddo," his dad said with a wink. "Superheroes are all around us. You just have to keep your eyes wide open." He whispered the last bit dramatically, stretching his eyes wide in a goofy way. Noah couldn't help it— he erupted into laughter, the sound filling the room.

That night, Noah tossed and turned, replaying his father's words in his mind. What did he mean? Where were all the superheroes? Surely, he would have noticed if they were around! Eventually, his eyelids drooped, and little by little, he drifted into a peaceful sleep.

The next day at school, Noah could hardly pay attention. He kept imagining himself wearing a bright red cape that flew behind him. His hands were on his hips, and he held his head high, just like the superheroes he dreamed of.

"Alright, class, today we're going to do something a little different," Mr. Wilson, Noah's English teacher, announced, snapping Noah out of his daydream. "Let's talk about the heroes in our lives." Noah's eyes lit up— finally, he could talk about superheroes!

Noah couldn't make up his mind as he tried to pick his favorite superhero. Would it be Ironman? Maybe the classic Superman? Or someone speedy like The Flash?

"Oh man, how can I pick just one?" Noah whispered to his best friend, James.

"I can't choose either," James frowned as he tried to pick his own favorite hero.

The other children excitedly yelled out their favorite heroes.

"Aquaman is my favorite!" Pierre said as he made a swimming motion through the air.

"No no! Black Panther is the best!" Tom insisted, slamming his hands on his desk to draw attention.

"Ghostrider! Ghostrider! You can't do better than that," Mikayla shouted excitedly, waving her arms in the air. "He's got fire."

"Yes, I can, actually. Try beating Spiderman!" Lola pretended to shoot webs out of her hands.

The squeaky, excited voices filled the room, growing louder with every second. Kids were shouting out names, each trying to convince the others that their superhero was the best.

Noah wasn't about to be left out. He joined in, yelling a whole bunch of his favorite superhero names.

Mr. Wilson finally had to calm the class down. "You've got lots of ideas now, which is awesome. Pick your favorite superhero and write a short paragraph explaining why you chose them. Any questions?"

Noah grew curious. He raised his hand and Mr. Wilson called on him.

"Mr. Wilson, do you have a favorite superhero?" The class went so silent you might have been able to hear a pin drop. Mr. Wilson closed his eyes and smiled.

"Why, yes I do, actually," he nodded. My favorite superhero... is my mom."

"Woah! Your mom's a superhero? Can I meet her?" Noah exclaimed. Mr. Wilson chuckled.

"Well, she's a superhero in a way. She's my superhero," he said. Before anyone could ask more questions, he told them to start their assignment.

The classroom filled with groans and frustrated sighs, but Noah wasn't upset like the others. Instead, he felt confused, just like he had the night before when talking with his dad.

"Why can't I see these superheroes? I've never seen one before..." Noah thought sadly as he and James walked toward the school courtyard.

Suddenly, Noah saw Billy, the biggest kid in school. Billy, an older student known for bullying younger kids, was at it again, this time picking on tiny Madison from first grade. Noah, like most kids in school, was afraid of Billy and stood frozen in place as he watched the bullying unfold. A crowd of students gathered. Noah quickly searched the area for a teacher, but no one was there to help

Noah watched Billy pull on Madison's pigtails. He wanted to help, but fear held him back, leaving him feeling powerless. His heart pounded in his chest.

"Silly piggy," Billy called Madison, causing the little girl's eyes to water. She started sobbing uncontrollably.

Unexpectedly, a voice yelled, "Stop it, Billy! Leave Madison alone!"

The crowd of kids parted, allowing someone to move forward. Noah saw the brave student who had spoken. It was Amber Kim, rolling up in her wheelchair. Billy just laughed, but it wasn't a nice laugh.

Oh no! Amber is new to this school. She doesn't know how scary Billy can be. He's like a monster! Noah thought, his eyes growing huge, his palms getting sweaty with fear.

"What do you want, wheelchair?" Billy teased, his words making a few kids gasp. But Amber didn't even blink. She sat there calmly, looking up at him without saying a word. Billy shifted uncomfortably, not sure what to do next.

"You know, Billy, my mom tells me that bullies are only bullies because they've got lots of hurt and sadness in their hearts," Amber told him.

"Why should I care what your mom says, hmm?" Billy challenged her. He crossed his arms over his chest and tapped his foot.

"Well, my mom *is* a psychologist," she said, her fingers tapping the armrest of her wheelchair.

"A psycho? That sounds about right. You must have gotten it from her," Billy laughed.

The crowd of students shook their heads at Billy's mean comment, but no one dared to step forward. They didn't want trouble with Billy. The whispers continued among the students and they waited to see how things would unfold.

"Not psycho. Psychologist. When I was little, she explained it to me this way. She's a *feelings doctor* and takes care of people who feel hurt on the inside instead of the outside," Amber explained while wrapping her arms around her body and giving herself a squeeze. "So my mom's a genius."

Billy's face turned as red as a tomato. He was so angry, he didn't even notice Madison sneaking away to hide behind Amber's wheelchair. Stomping over to Amber, Billy raised his arm like he was going to hit her.

But Amber quickly put her hands up and shouted, "No, stop it, Billy!"

This time, Billy froze, scared that a teacher might have heard. He didn't want to get in trouble—his parents were very strict. He looked around nervously when Amber suddenly spoke up again.

"Billy, I'm sorry that you're feeling sad and mad. I'm here if you ever want to talk. But it's not okay to hurt other kids because of how you feel. You look silly when you bully people," Amber said calmly. Billy looked down, embarrassed—no one had ever talked to him like that before.

From where he stood, Noah noticed a few things. Billy looked like he felt a little bad about what he did. And Madison, along with everyone else, was looking at Amber with admiration. It reminded Noah of the way people look at Superman after he saves the day.

At that moment, Noah finally understood what his dad meant. Not all superheroes wear capes or fly or shoot lasers from their eyes. Some stay right here on the ground, and they can be friends or even strangers.

That night, Noah had a lot to share during dinner.

"It was so cool! Billy even said sorry after," Noah said, stuffing a big spoonful of mac and cheese into his mouth. His parents looked at each other and laughed.

"Is that right? So, do you see superheroes now?" his dad asked, wiping sauce from his mustache.

"You're right, dad. They're all around us. Everywhere," he informed his parents. With a big grin, he said, "I'm going to be a superhero just like Amber someday!"

> *Noah's story shows us that being a superhero isn't about having super strength or speed, but about standing up for what's right and being kind. Even though Amber wasn't big or powerful, she showed true courage by standing up to a bully and protecting Madison. This teaches us that real heroes, no matter how big or small they are, are the ones who help others, and that bravery comes from doing the right thing, even when it's hard.*

The Reckless Racer

The sun shone brightly over the small town of Elmwood Grove. It was here that 12 year old Evan could often be seen zipping past on his bright red bike.

Ever since he was a little boy, Evan has always loved bike races. He started out with an itty-bitty little tricycle that his parents gifted him on his fourth birthday. Then, he got a bicycle with training wheels. Eventually, those training wheels came off and Evan's passion for bike racing grew stronger than ever.

Everyone in town knew Evan. When people heard his name, they'd say, "Oh, that's the boy with the bike."

"The child has so much talent, don't you think, Geraldine?" his aunt had once said to his mother, watching him race around.

It was true! Evan, though still quite young, had somehow managed to teach himself all sorts of tricks. He could do a front and back wheelie and took great pride in it.

The more tricks Evan learned, the more he swelled with pride. People cheered for him, and he loved it. Soon, he started doing riskier and more dangerous stunts.

His mother tried to get him to stop. At first, she spoke gently, "Evan, sweetie, those stunts are really dangerous. I'm worried about you." She sat him down and explained how risky his tricks were.

Evan heard her, but he didn't listen. He rushed out the door that evening and showed off more stunts to his neighbors and friends. His riding became more and more unsafe.

As Evan's stunts got wilder, his mom's warnings got louder. "Evan Baxter, if you don't stop right now, you'll be grounded until you leave for college!" she yelled, her face filled with worry.

This got his attention. He rode his bike around safely for a while in the evenings. But there was no fun, no thrill to his days anymore.

Evan spent the whole week complaining to his mom, hoping she'd change her mind, but she didn't. He was unhappy and made sure she knew it by grumbling and not talking to her whenever they crossed paths.

Knock, knock, knock! Someone was at the front door.

"Who could that be?" his mom whispered as she dried her hands on her apron and opened the door. Standing there was Patricia, their neighbor, holding her tiny Chihuahua.

"Geraldine, I hope this isn't a bad time. I wanted to drop this off," Patricia said with a big smile, handing Evan's mom a flyer while scooping her dog up into her arms. The Chihuahua let out a squeaky bark.

"What's this?" Evan's mom asked, taking the flyer.

"It's a bike race! I thought Evan might be interested," Patricia said, leaning in like it was a secret. "Anyway, I've got to run. I've got a casserole in the oven."

"Take care!" his mom called as Patricia waved and hurried back to her house.

Evan, who had been eavesdropping the whole time, ran out and begged to join the race.

"You haven't even seen the details yet," his mom said, putting the flyer down neatly on the table and heading back to the kitchen.

Evan grabbed the flyer, his eyes scanning every word—except for the part about the $50 entrance fee.

"Mom, this looks amazing! It's on a weekend so I don't have to miss school either. Also, did you see this part?" he asked, pointing to a corner of the flyer. "Grand prize $200!"

"Did you see the entrance fee, though, sweetie?" his mom asked while intently dropping spices into the dish she was preparing.

E Evan groaned. "It's only $50, Mom. Please," he said, begging and listing every reason he could think of as to why he just had to join the race. His mom stayed quiet, listening.

"Fifty dollars is a lot of money for us right now, Evan. And there's no guarantee we'll win $200," she said. Evan's shoulders drooped, and his face fell. "But, I know how much you love racing, and you've been better about racing safely. Let's go ahead and get your name on the list!"

Evan's eyes went wide with surprise. "Really? You mean it, Mom?" he asked, barely able to believe it.

His mother nodded, smiling down at her son as she ruffled his hair. Evan cheered and jumped around with excitement, then hugged his mom tightly.

"But–" Evan's mother suddenly interrupted his celebration, "–you have to promise that you're not going to do anything dangerous." Her face turned serious. Evan gulped. His mom was usually kind and gentle, but she could be really scary when she needed to be.

"I promise," Evan said with a confident nod. Surely, he could hold off on the cool stunts for a while.

The race was a month away, and Evan spent every spare second practicing. He wanted nothing more than to win. Everyone knew him as "Lightning Evan," and losing would be way too embarrassing.

After school, he'd rush home, complete his homework, and run straight over to his red bike parked in the garage. He practiced at least an hour each day, sometimes even before school.

He also took great care of his bike, oiling the chains and keeping it bright and shiny for race day. "I'm keeping it squeaky clean so it'll look good in the pictures," he told his mother with a grin.

"The pictures?" she asked.

"Yeah! You know, the pictures people will take when I win! Maybe they'll put me in the newspaper!" Evan scratched the back of his head, already imagining his big victory.

He was sure he'd win, no question about it. There was no competition. Until one day, his classmates, Peter and Luna, told him something that made his legs shake for the first time.

"Did you hear about the new kid in the neighborhood?" Peter asked during lunch.

"No, who?" Evan said through a mouthful of tuna sandwich.

"He's a transfer student. Wait! There he is now!" Luna called while pointing at a tall boy with pale skin and short, straight hair.

"My mom says he's from Japan. I talked to him earlier, and he's really nice. His name's Yura. I bet you two would get along," Peter said.

"Oh? Why?" Evan asked.

"He's a bike racer too. You might see him at the race this weekend," Luna said

Evan got up, stuffed his hands in his pockets, and looked at Yura. He seemed nice with a big smile and hearty laugh. Lots of students crowded around him, listening to his stories from Japan—especially the ones about how he'd won so many bike races.

As the days passed, whenever Evan walked by, kids whispered about him in the hallway. The same thing happened in class, while waiting for the bus, and even when he went on his evening bike ride. Evan grew quieter, and a sick feeling started to grow in his stomach. He was more worried than he'd ever been.

What if I don't win? he thought, riding through the neighborhood, not paying attention. He almost knocked over poor Mrs. Fitzgerald, his ninety-year-old neighbor. She gave him a mean look, and he yelled out an apology, panicking.

That night, after dinner, Evan went straight to his room. He skipped his usual evening talks with his mom, saying he had homework to do. The race was the next day, and it was all anyone at school could talk about.

Evan became more determined than ever to win, and that's when he had his first bad idea. He decided to cheat. He stayed up late, under his blanket with a flashlight, pencil, and notebook, mapping out the race route.

But he knew a shortcut—at the corner right between Darby Street and Springhill Lane.

I'll never lose to anyone! He whispered to himself, voice full of determination and passion.

Whenever he heard his mom coming, he turned off the flashlight and pretended to be asleep. By 3 a.m., he had memorized the route, tossed the paper in the trash, and finally went to bed.

The day of the race finally came and everyone gathered at the starting line to see the contestants off. Peter and Luna were there to cheer for Evan. But Evan's eyes were fixed on Yura.

Yura was smiling and laughing with his friends while the other racers warmed up and checked their bikes one last time. Evan thought it would be nice to wish Yura good luck before the race, so he walked over to introduce himself.

"Hey, I'm Evan," he said with a smile. Yura turned around, beaming.

"Evan! I've heard a lot about you," Yura said, shaking his hand. "Good luck in the race!"

The happiness in Yura's voice made Evan second-guess his plan. Yura didn't seem like he cared about beating him—he was just having fun. Evan almost decided not to cheat. Almost.

"On your marks!" the official, Peter's dad, shouted into the megaphone. All the racers stood straight at the starting line, eyes focused on the road ahead.

"Get set!" Evan's heart pounded in his chest. This was really happening.

"Go!" With that, the entire line of racers sped off, their bikes disappearing in a flash. Behind them, the crowd cheered wildly. As Evan sped away, the sound got softer and softer and then wasn't there at all.

Evan was leading the race with the other racers far behind him. He felt his confidence come back and pedaled even faster. He swooshed through each turn and checkpoint effortlessly. His bike was handling perfectly.

All of a sudden, without warning, Yura zoomed past him with a polite, toothy. Evan leaned forward on his bike, pedaling faster than he ever had before. His legs were going numb, but he couldn't overtake Yura. Yura had soared far ahead.

Then, Evan remembered his plan. He scanned the bushes and trees, looking for the shortcut he had planned out the night before. Suddenly, he saw it!

Without a second glance, Evan turned off the main path and rode onto the trail. It was darker than he remembered, with thick bushes and roots sticking up everywhere. It felt strange and a little scary, but he kept going. All he could think about was winning.

Suddenly, a loud snap echoed through the woods and Evan found himself tumbling down a steep slope. He kept falling as he grabbed for roots and vines, but they broke in his hands. He felt dizzy as he tumbled down, and when he finally hit the ground, the world went black.

* * *

The next thing Evan heard was his mom crying and lots of voices he didn't recognize. He tried to open his eyes, but the light was too bright, so he quickly shut them again.

Slowly, he got used to the light and opened his eyes. He sat up and looked around an unfamiliar room. The first thing he did was search for his mom, who he found sleeping in a chair next to him.

"Mom," he called softly as she stirred awake.

"Oh, baby! You're finally awake!" she cried, jumping up and hugging him tightly.

"What happened, Mom? My legs hurt," he said, feeling confused. He cried out as a sharp pain shot through his knee.

"Don't move, sweetie. You took a tumble during the race and fell into a pit. Luckily, an old couple was walking by and saw you. That's how we found you. But you broke your leg."

Evan threw the blanket off and saw his right leg wrapped in a thick, white cast.

Evan felt his heart sink. Not only did he lose the race, but he wouldn't get to compete in any more races this season. He hung his head in sadness and shame. Tears streamed down his cheeks and he sniffled, trying to hold them back.

"I'm sorry, mom," he apologized, realizing how worried she must have been.

His mom didn't say anything right away, which made Evan think she was mad at him. Maybe she was, but she loved him even more. She leaned down and gave him a gentle kiss on the top of his head.

Evan looked up and saw her smiling. "I'm definitely upset that you did something so dangerous, but I think not being able to race is already a big enough punishment."

"I should've listened to you! You warned me not to do dangerous stuff, and now I can't even race my bike because I didn't listen to what you said!" Evan cried as he hugged his mom tightly.

"Well, let this be a lesson," his mom said softly. "We just want you to stay safe, sweetheart. That's why we give you advice, not to stop your fun, but to protect you."

Evan nodded and made a promise to himself. From now on, he would be more careful and follow the rules. Cool tricks might be fun, but they weren't worth getting hurt over.

Evan's story teaches us that sometimes our desire to win or impress others can lead to poor decisions. At first, Evan was determined to win the race, even if it meant cheating and taking dangerous risks. But when he got hurt, he realized that being safe and following the rules is much more important than winning at any cost. This story reminds us that our safety and well-being should always come first, and that shortcuts can lead to unexpected consequences.

The Littlest Explorer

"Alright kids, has everyone got their permission slips?" Mr. Wilson called from the front of the class, waving a piece of paper in the air.

"Yes!" the students called in a sing-song way, their little fingers gripping tightly onto similar looking papers.

The kids of class 2A were due to go on a camping trip the following weekend. It was a two-day, one-night stay in one of Florida's camping forests.

The children were absolutely thrilled, as most eight-year-olds would be. Many of them had never been camping before and the ones that had talked a great deal about it. Everyone was grinning from ear to ear, except little Marcus Ng.

Marcus adjusted his thick glasses on the bridge of his nose and looked around. He had never gone anywhere without his parents and wasn't sure if he wanted to now. He frowned, his hands hidden inside his oversized sweater.

"I can't wait! Maybe we'll see bears! The big white ones!" Noah shouted, making his fingers into claws and growling at his friends.

"Those are called polar bears, Noah. And I doubt we'll be seeing any in these parts. They live in the Arctic," Mr. Wilson chuckled as he explained.

"What about vampires? My cousin said she saw lots of vampires flying around when she went camping!" Gabe asked. Mr. Wilson looked up at him and burst out laughing.

"I think she was teasing you," Mr. Wilson said, still smiling.

"No no! She said they were flying and they were the size of fat cats," Gabe insisted.

"Well those might have been vampire bats. Not vampires. In my thirty-two years on this Earth, I've never known anyone who came about a vampire," Mr. Wilson said with a shake of his head. "Now stop scaring the rest of the class."

Marcus wasn't all too fond of big white bears or vampires—whether they were bats or not! He sunk down in his seat and thought of ways he might be able to skip out on the camping trip.

"Mr. Wilson?" Marcus called with his hand only half in the air.

"Yes, Marcus?"

"If we get sick the day of the camp, will we still have to go?" he asked, thinking of excuses but knowing full well that his parents would never pass on the chance for him to be social and gain some real world experience.

Mr. Wilson put his book down and sat at the front of his desk with one eyebrow higher than the other. "Are you planning on being sick that day?" he questioned the nervous boy.

Marcus fidgeted with the sleeves of his sweater and mumbled a quiet no before slumping down and putting his head on his desk. Mr. Wilson smiled warmly.

"It'll be alright, Marcus. You'll see. Once we get there, it's going to be fun," Mr. Wilson said, trying to cheer him up, but Marcus wasn't so sure. He was still worried about things like bears and scary creatures.

The rest of the day flew by with more talk about the camping trip. Marcus walked through the hallways and heard Melissa talking about wanting to meet Bigfoot. Another classmate, Sonya, said she heard they were only going to be given earthworms during mealtime. The worst rumor was from Jacob, who said that teachers would leave naughty kids in the jungle and head back to school without them!

The bus ride home was no better. Noah said that the kids that went on the school trip last year all got eaten by mummies.

"Aren't mummies supposed to be in Egypt?" Sonya asked while scratching her head.

"Yeah. So?" Noah retorted.

"So why would they be on our camping trip?"

Noah gulped, looking nervous. He didn't have an answer.

"May... maybe the mummies took a plane here?" Marcus stuttered.

"Oh, don't be silly, Marcus. *Everyone* knows mummies aren't allowed on airplanes!" Gabe called from the back of the bus. "Besides, they don't even have mouths to eat us."

Marcus didn't want to join the conversation anymore. In his mind, he had decided that going on this camping trip meant that he would meet Bigfoot and be eaten by mummies. He was absolutely shaking in fear.

When Marcus got off the bus, things didn't get any better. He spent the rest of the day hiding in his room, crying in the shower, and refusing to tell his mom anything.

Worried about Marcus's strange behavior, Marcus's mom sent his older brother, Peter to try to find out what might be bothering him.

"Peter, could you check on your brother?" she asked, resting her chin on her hand, her eyebrows furrowed with worry.

Peter didn't ask any questions. The moment his mother told him about his younger brother, he went straight to Marcus's room, knocked three times, and waited.

Knock, knock, knock.

No answer. Peter knocked again, this time louder.

KNOCK, KNOCK, KNOCK!

Still no answer. Peter pressed his ear against the cold door and heard quiet sobbing.

"Marcus! I'm coming in!" Peter called as he opened the door and stepped into the dark room.

He switched on the lights and noticed streaks of tears staining Marcus's face. Peter rushed over and hugged his little brother, and Marcus held onto him, crying. Peter patted Marcus' back gently to calm him down.

When Marcus was only sniffling, Peter pulled away and asked, "What's wrong? Is someone bothering you at school?"

Marcus didn't say anything. He reached into his bag and handed Peter the permission slip for the camping trip.

Peter took it, read it, and his eyes lit up. "Oh! You're going on the school trip? I remember my trip when I was your age! It was four years ago, and—"

"You went on the school trip?" Marcus interrupted, looking surprised.

Peter nodded. "Of course I did. It was fun!" he said, smiling as he remembered his own trip.

"How come the mummies didn't eat you?" Marcus asked, tilting his head in confusion.

Peter looked shocked. "What do you mean?" he asked.

"Well, Noah said there were mummies that flew all the way from Egypt to eat us. And then Sonya said we'd have to eat worms for dinner!" Marcus said, starting to cry again, but stopped when Peter started to chuckle.

"No, nothing like that happens at camp, Marcus. Your teachers are going to take very good care of you. And after dinner, you get to sit around a campfire and roast marshmallows. No one's going to make you eat worms," Peter giggled.

"Really?" Marcus asked. He should've been happy but he was still uncertain.

"You know? I've never really known you to be scared of these sorts of things. Maybe you're just anxious about going on the trip?" Peter asked, looking closely at his brother.

"An–shios? What's that?" Marcus tried to sound it out and Peter giggled as he patted his head.

"Anxious," Peter repeated slower this time. "It's a funny feeling you get in your tummy sometimes when you're scared or nervous."

Marcus made an "O" shape with his mouth but didn't say anything. He thought about it while Peter waited. After a moment, Marcus nodded slowly.

"I think I am—anxious," he looked to his brother. Peter nodded. "I've never been away from you, mom, and dad before. Not for *two whole days!* And what if a bear does eat me?" Marcus cried.

Peter smiled softly at him, patting his head. "You're not going to get eaten by anything. I felt the same way on my first camping trip too. I missed you, mom, and dad even before I left. But you know how I got over it?" Peter whispered like it was a secret. Marcus shook his head.

"I brought a tiny notebook along and wrote down everything I wanted to tell you guys back home."

Marcus leaned back and thought about it. It was a good idea! Writing in a notebook would help him feel better. He relaxed for awhile as Peter told him stories about his own camping trip.

Finally, with a big smile on his face, Marcus walked downstairs with his brother and gave his mother the permission slip. She was more than happy to sign it.

Marcus and his parents went shopping for everything Marcus would need for camp and didn't forget to get him a small purple notebook. It was tiny enough to fit in his pocket, with a pen attached by a string of purple beads.

The day of the camping trip came finally came, and Marcus felt a little nervous during the bus ride to the camp site. He pulled out his notebook and scribbled in messy handwriting: *The bus ride is a bit scary, but I like hearing the stories people are telling. I'm sitting next to my best friend, Hunter. I miss you mom, dad, and Peter!*

He put his notebook away, and soon they arrived at the campsite. The games and activities started right away, and Marcus made sure to write everything down:

I learned how to put up a tent. Mr. Wilson says that I'm a natural. I also found a lost compass.

Noah went looking for bears but found a squirrel instead. He scared it. It was hurt so we took care of it and named it Chocolate because of its fluffy, brown tail.

I caught a fish today! Just like dad! It scared me a little, so I don't think I'll be going fishing again.

Melissa told a campfire story about big spiders in the forest waiting to get us. But I wasn't scared at all!

Pretty soon, his notebook was filled with all sorts of stories and he couldn't wait to get home to share them. His friends liked his notebook idea and even tried to write their stories on leaves. Mr. Wilson praised Marcus for the excellent idea. Marcus grinned and said, "It was all my brother's idea."

Before the trip ended and they had to leave, Marcus crouched down next to a big rock and got his notebook out for one last entry.

It said: *I had lots of fun! Thanks, Peter! I can't wait to get home and tell you everything. I miss you all. See you soon! Love, Marcus.*

Marcus's story shows us that it's normal to feel nervous about trying new things, but sometimes facing our fears can lead to great experiences. At first, Marcus was scared of going camping and imagined all sorts of things going wrong. But with the support of his brother, Peter, and by writing down his thoughts in a notebook, Marcus overcame his worries and ended up having a fun adventure. This story shows us that when we face our fears and try new things, we often discover that they aren't as scary as we thought—and we can even have fun along the way.

The Jealous Friend

Crestview Elementary was famous for many things. There was their taekwondo team, their junior badminton players, and their melodious choir. But the one thing it was most famous for was its soccer team.

Juan was one of the players on the team. He joined the team two years ago when he was only eight years old.

He had actually started showing a passion for soccer from an even younger age. The moment he could walk, he started kicking things around. So his mother bought him a blue rubber ball that was made for kids. Juan loved it with all his heart. He never went anywhere without his favorite blue ball.

One day at the park, he saw a group of high school boys kicking and chasing after a ball, a lot like he did. He stopped playing, sat on the grass, and watched intently while the older boys played. His keen interest and curiosity didn't go unnoticed by his parents.

Later, he asked his parents what those boys were playing and found out it was a sport called soccer. From that day onwards, Juan was passionate about soccer.

Today, Juan had just finished playing another big game for his school, and Crestview Elementary had won! Everyone was cheering—the students, the parents, and the teachers. But Juan didn't feel happy. His face was red, and not just from running around. The cheering went on and no one noticed that he was upset. Juan became more and more cross. His face twisted into an unpleasant frown.

As the team gathered, the coach and other players praised Juan's best friend, Ricardo, for scoring the winning goal.

"Good job, Ricardo!" Coach called while they walked up to the benches.

"That was amazing!" one of their teammates cheered.

"What would we have done without you, Ricardo? That shot was legendary!" the team's goalkeeper shouted happily.

Juan and Ricardo had been best friends since they were still in diapers. They always played together, and as they grew up, they started sharing the same hobbies. At first, Juan loved it because they could spend even more time together after school. But today, Juan wasn't happy at all.

You see, Juan was the first to love soccer and Ricardo only started playing after Juan introduced him to it. Juan taught Ricardo many of the tricks he knew. Now, watching Ricardo score the winning goal, something new and uncomfortable bubbled up in Juan's stomach.

"Juan, Juan! Did you see that? Did you see how I scored the goal?" Ricardo called out while jogging towards his best friend. Juan gave him an unpleasant glare.

"Yeah, I saw. You used the move I taught you." Juan said unenthusiastically, not even looking at Ricardo.

"Oh, right! I guess I did. Thanks, amigo!" Ricardo said, moving closer to pat Juan on the back, but Juan stepped away. Ricardo's smile faded, and his eyebrows lowered in confusion.

Coach noticed Juan's angry face and asked, "What's wrong, Juan?"

By now, other players had gathered around. Ricardo was silent, trying to figure out why Juan was so upset. Everyone was confused.

All of a sudden, Juan shouted angrily, "I was supposed to score the winning goal. Me! Not you!" he yelled while pointing a finger at Ricardo. Ricardo was shocked and didn't say anything. He didn't understand why his friend was so angry.

"But we won, I don't understand why you're so mad," Ricardo whispered.

"That was supposed to be my winning kick. Not yours. I passed the ball to you!" Juan yelled in frustration. Tears welled in his eyes.

"Exactly. You passed me the ball, so I kicked it into the goal and we won," Ricardo explained, still confused.

Juan got more furious. He clenched his small fists by his side and shouted, "You were supposed to pass it back to me. That was my winning kick and you stole it!" And with that, Juan ran off the field, upset.

He kept running until his legs got tired. When he finally stopped, he realized he had run halfway home. As he walked the rest of the way, he kept thinking about how angry he was at Ricardo. *How dare he score the winning goal when I'm the one who introduced him to soccer!*

Juan thought of all the ways he wanted to hate Ricardo. But suddenly, memories of all the fun he and Ricardo had shared came back to him. Slowly, his anger started to fade, and he began to feel something else—guilt.

He was starting to feel bad for how he acted. He didn't even congratulate Ricardo on his victory, and he knew he ruined the team's celebration. He felt very ashamed of himself. He was also worried he had lost his best friend.

When he got home, he took a deep breath in and decide to talk to his parents. He always went to them for advice when he didn't know what to do. They always knew just what to say.

"Mom...Dad," he called nervously. His parents, who had just gotten home, looked at him. Juan suddenly felt more nervous than before. He wasn't sure how they would react—would they be upset? Or disappointed?

"Juan! Is the game over already? How was it?" his mother asked, clapping her hands with excitement.

"I bet your team won, right?" his father asked confidently.

Juan nodded weakly but didn't look up to meet his parents' eyes. He didn't cheer or ask for a snack like he usually did after winning a game. Instead, he just stood there, frowning and avoiding eye contact.

"Something happened after the game, and I want--" Juan started, but a knock at the door interrupted him.

"Hold on, sweetie," his mom said as she went to answer the door. Juan stood in silence and fidgeted with his fingers. He didn't know how to tell his parents without sounding like a bully.

"Juan, there you are, bud! I've been searching all over for you," a familiar gruff voice called from behind him. Juan turned to see Coach, who looked relieved.

"What's going on?" Juan's father asked as he walked over from the table.

"Juan had a little argument with Ricardo after the game and ran off," Coach explained. "We got worried when we couldn't find him."

"With Ricardo? But they're such good friends," Juan's mother said, surprised.

Coach looked over at Juan and raised his eyebrows as if saying, *do you want to tell them or should I?* Juan thought for a second and took another deep breath.

"I got mad at Ricardo during the game. He was supposed to pass the ball to me so I could score the winning goal, but he scored it himself instead. Everyone was praising him and cheering his name," Juan explained.

His parents listened quietly, and his mom knelt down to his level, rubbing soothing circles on his back. "Go on, sweetheart," she said softly.

"I just didn't like it that he joined the team because of me, but now he's in the spotlight, and I can't do anything for the team," he admitted through pouted lips while fighting back tears.

The adults looked at each other and stayed silent for a moment, trying to understand the situation. They thought for a long time, thinking carefully about what to say. Coach finally broke the silence.

"Juan, you know you're a fantastic player, right? And that the team is lucky to have you?" Juan shrugged.

Coach then continued, "Most people think that the only players who make a difference on the team are the strikers. But you're smart. You know soccer is more than that. What do you think about the other positions on the field?"

Juan thought about it. He pictured all the players and what they did during the game.

"The striker is important to score goals. But other positions are important too. The goalkeeper keeps our opponents from scoring a goal in our goalpost. The defense tries to steal the ball from the other team so they can't score a goal at all. Everyone has a purpose on the field." As he explained, he realized that he had it all wrong. It wasn't just one person who made them win—it was teamwork.

"There's no 'I' in team, son," his dad said, and Juan nodded.

"What about Ricardo? I yelled at him really badly earlier. What if he doesn't want to be my friend anymore? I don't think he's ever going to want to talk to me again."

Juan's mom hugged him tightly. "Don't worry, sweetie," she said. "I'm sure Ricardo will understand, but you need to apologize first."

When Monday came, Juan knew it was his chance to fix things. He walked around the school looking for Ricardo, but he wasn't waiting by the lockers like usual. Juan started to feel even more guilty and nervous about talking to him.

Just as the bell rang, Juan spotted Ricardo walking into their first class— English with Mr. Hendrick, who was always a few minutes late. Juan saw this as his chance to clear things up with Ricardo.

"Hey, Ricardo," Juan said, sitting down next to him. Ricardo looked a bit shocked but said hello back. They sat quietly for a moment, neither of them knowing what to say.

Juan was the one who broke the silence. "Ricardo, I'm sorry for how I acted the other day. I don't know what came over me. I guess I was a bit frustrated, that's all."

Ricardo thought for a second. Then, he smiled at Juan. "It's okay, it was a mistake. I understand."

The apology went smoothly, and soon the boys were back to laughing and joking around like usual.

Juan didn't forget the lesson he had learned. He started trying out different positions on the soccer field and discovered that he was really good at defense. He wasn't jealous of his teammates' wins anymore because he knew that a win for the team was a win for everyone.

He realized that working together and supporting his friends was what really mattered. Winning as a team felt a lot better than winning alone.

Juan's story shows us that it's easy to feel jealous when someone else gets recognition, but true friendship and teamwork mean celebrating each other's successes. Juan learned that it wasn't about who scored the winning goal—it was about how everyone played a part in the victory. By realizing that every player on the team is important, Juan discovered that winning together feels better than focusing on individual achievements. This reminds us to support and cheer for our friends, knowing that their success is a win for everyone.

The Careless Student

"Go, go, go! To your left!" Jay called out in exasperation.

"Your left or my left?" Ben yelled back in confusion and panic.

"We have the same left, Ben!" Jay yelled back.

The pair of eleven-year-olds had arrived home from school and sat themselves down to play a series of video games. They started with *Mario Kart*, then moved on to *Call of Duty*.

It was almost dinner time. Ben had mentioned a few times that they had piles of homework to do for tomorrow, but Jay wasn't worried. He never worried about homework.

"Ben, your mom just called," Jay's mom said from the kitchen as she peeled potatoes for dinner. "She said to let you know that if you aren't back in the next fifteen minutes, she won't let you visit Jay after school anymore."

Ben gasped and scrambled to his feet, tossing the game controller to the side and rushing out. He yelled a quick goodbye to Jay as he rushed out the door and reminded him not to forget about his homework.

Jay pretended he didn't hear his friend and carried on playing. His mother— who had warned him at least three times to get started on his homework— was growing more and more frustrated. This had become the routine in their house.

Jay always came home from school, grabbed a quick snack, and started playing video games. His mother constantly nagged at him to do his homework and study for his tests, but he never listened.

"I don't *need* to study, mom. You know I'm a quick learner," Jay would say when his mom sent him to his room to study before a big test.

When she asked him to do his homework, he'd reply, "Don't worry, Mom. I'll get to it. It's super easy."

Jay was extremely confident because he always managed to get decent grades, so he didn't think he needed to change. But his mom kept reminding him that luck wouldn't always be on his side.

"You know the story of the hare and the tortoise, don't you, Jay? Well, just remember that even though the hare was definitely supposed to win that race, he lost to the tortoise because of his overconfidence."

Jay yawned and barely listened.

On the bus the next morning, Jay had his homework on his lap. He was only beginning to get it done. Ben glanced from his seat and saw what Jay was doing.

"I reminded you to do it *yesterday*," Ben muttered with a disappointed shake of his head.

"Yeah, but remember," Jay paused dramatically. "I'm a genius," he added, tapping his pencil against his head.

It was difficult to write down his answers because of the bumpy bus ride, but eventually, he finished.

"Done!" he announced while stuffing the paper into his school bag and tossing it to the side. He shut his eyes and leaned back in his seat while Ben stared at him.

"You really finished? It took me an hour to do all of it," Ben said.

From the seat in front of them, another one of their classmates, who overheard their conversation, agreed. And so did the girl beside her. They were amazed at how quickly Jay managed to finish the homework.

Jay just grinned. He always scored decent grades while submitting last minute work and not studying at all. So he felt like there was no need to study and put in any extra effort if he was just going to do well in the class anyway.

Their first lesson of the day was a science lesson. The students handed in their homework to Mr. Turner, who said they would be starting a new topic—cells.

Most of the students were really interested in the lesson. They took notes and tried their best to draw the plant cell like Mr. Turner did on the board. They struggled to understand at first but eventually did, and lots of questions were asked and answered.

Jay, on the other hand, was busy doodling video game characters and only half listening. He used to pay attention in class, but lately, since he'd been getting good grades without much effort, he thought fifth-grade subjects were too easy for him.

"The mitochondria is also known as the..." Mr. Turner paused to allow the students to answer the question.

"...powerhouse of the cell!" the majority yelled in unison while some mumbled it under their breath. Jay was the only one who hadn't answered. He didn't even hear the question. Mr. Turner noticed but didn't say anything because the bell rang, and everyone rushed off to their next class.

"I'll have your midterms and homework graded by tomorrow!" Mr. Turner called after the students.

The next day, Jay looked terrible. He kept nodding off in class, had dark circles under his eyes, and his skin looked pale. His hair was a mess too. He was exhausted.

"What happened to you?" Ben asked as he took a seat next to Jay.

Jay beamed at him and explained, "I was building a new house in Minecraft."

He went on to explain every detail of the pretend house. He also talked about how he got a new pet wolf in the game.

"A wolf? I didn't know you could do that in Minecraft," Ben said, taking his books out before Mr. Turner came in.

"Of course you didn't. I know because I'm a genius," Jay said, tapping a pencil on his head. "I just gave them some bones I found in the game and..." Jay kept talking, but Ben stopped listening.

Most of the students—except for Jay—were really nervous because Mr. Turner was going to hand back their midterm test grades.

Ben was tapping his foot absent-mindedly, Evelyn was humming a tune, and Poppy was making little origami cranes. Everyone had their own way of staying calm, but Jay was getting annoyed.

"He's only giving us back our test results, but you're all acting like the dentist is coming in to yank out a tooth," Jay grumbled.

Poppy turned around, annoyed. "Some of us studied really hard for this test. Of course we're nervous, Jay," she snapped at him.

Amir was frowning, too. "Yeah, not all of us were born geniuses," he said. Jay wasn't bothered at all. He shrugged and continued doodling on his paper.

"Good morning, class!" Mr. Turner called as he walked in. Everyone fixed themselves to their seats and stiffly waited as he passed out the tests. The room buzzed with excitement as students got their scores.

"Yes! I got an A!" Poppy shouted, high-fiving Ben, who also got an A.

"I got a B!" Evelyn said proudly. She usually struggled in Science, so she was happy with her grade.

Eventually, Jay's name was called and he strolled to the front to collect his results. Mr. Turner folded the paper in half as he handed it to him, which was strange because he didn't do that for anyone else. Back at his seat, Jay opened the paper.

His heart sank. A big F was written in bright red ink next to a short instruction: *See me after class.* He quickly folded the paper again, but William, who sat behind him, had already seen.

"Hey, did you fail, Jay?" William said loudly, making sure the whole class heard.

Everyone turned to look at Jay. Feeling embarrassed, he pulled his hoodie over his head and stared down at his desk for the rest of the class.

After the bell rang, Jay dragged his feet to Mr. Turner's desk. "Ah, Jay. Just the person I wanted to see," he said, still searching for something in a box next to his desk. His face twisted into a curious one as he felt around.

"Why did you fail me, Mr. Turner?" Jay asked, upset. He had never gotten anything lower than a B-minus before.

Jay flipped the test and realized he had missed an entire page of questions. He hadn't even seen them. Worse, when he checked the questions he *did* answer, most of them were wrong. His head spun, and he sat down in a nearby chair, confused.

"I see you've only just checked your answers?" Mr. Turner asked. Jay nodded, his eyes still staring at the big F at the top of his test.

"How did this happen?" Jay mumbled to himself. Mr. Turner suddenly started quizzing Jay.

"Jay, what's the fourth color of the rainbow?"

Jay thought for a while, recalling the pattern in his head. *Red, orange, yellow, green.* "It's green," he answered.

"Good, and what's the process called that enables ice to change to water?" the teacher asked.

"Ice to water? That's called melting," Jay answered more quickly.

"Alright, one last question, a snake is classified as a..." he looked at Jay intently with one eyebrow raised.

"A reptile. What does this have to do with anything, Mr. Turner?" Jay asked, gripping his test paper tightly. The teacher frowned.

"Jay, those are the same questions from the test that you got wrong. But you know the answers! You made careless mistakes."

Jay's mouth dropped open as he looked back at his test. It was true. For the rainbow question, he had written down orange. For the ice-to-water question, he had written freezing instead of melting. And for the snake question, he had written amphibian instead of reptile.

"You're right. I do know the answers... They're all careless mistakes," Jay realized with a gasp.

Mr. Turner patted Jay on the shoulder. "Have you been distracted lately? Sometimes, even when your body is here, your mind can be somewhere else. That can lead to mistakes."

Jay thought for a second, then groaned. "I was playing a new video game the night before, and it was so cool. During the test, I couldn't get it out of my head. The only thing I kept thinking about was how excited I was to get done with school, go home, and start playing the game again."

Mr. Turner didn't scold Jay or get mad. Instead, he pulled out a book called *Time Management for Beginners* and handed it to him. Jay took it quietly, flipping through the pages. When he was done, he looked up at Mr. Turner with curiosity.

"Believe it or not, I had the same problem when I was your age," Mr. Turner said. "A teacher gave me this book and told me it would change my life. Now, Jay, I want to give it to you."

Jay felt like he might cry but held it back. He stood up straight and nodded to Mr. Turner. It was a silent promise that he would change his habits and try to be more responsible.

Something about the confidence in Mr. Turner's eyes made Jay *want* to change his ways. It felt nice to have someone believe in him.

At home, Jay got a talking-to from his parents about the bad grade, but he accepted it. He understood that it was a consequence of his own actions. Later that night, his mom found him asleep earlier than usual. Placed neatly on his desk was a new daily schedule he created out of markers and highlighters. Next to it was the book Mr. Turner had given him.

Over the next month, Jay changed a lot. He still played video games to relax, but he limited it to just one hour a day—even on weekends! Instead, Jay spent more time studying, helping around the house, and finding new hobbies. He was very careful about following his schedule and even carried it in his folder wherever he went.

It was time to get their final exam results. Just like before, Mr. Turner called out everyone's name one by one. Just like before, Mr. Turner called out everyone's names one by one. The longer Jay's name wasn't called, the more worried he became.

Could it be possible that I failed again? He thought sadly.

"And last but not least, give a big round of applause for our tiny legend, Jay!" Mr. Turner lifted his test paper up and a big A+ was written at the top. Everyone clapped and congratulated him.

"Congratulations, Jay!" Ben said with a pat on Jay's back.

"Thank you, everyone. And thank you, Mr. Turner, for believing in me."

Jay kept the old test with the failing grade stored neatly in his room. He also pinned up the new test with his top score right next to it. The grades were a reminder to him that putting in effort, discipline, and doing the right thing would always lead to better results.

Jay's story teaches us that overconfidence and neglecting our responsibilities can lead to unexpected consequences. At first, Jay thought he could succeed without putting in effort, but when he failed his test, he realized that even smart people make mistakes when they don't focus or prepare. By learning the importance of time management and discipline, Jay turned his habits around and succeeded. This story reminds us that success isn't just about talent; it's about hard work and dedication.

The Recipe Book

D iego could hardly wait for five o'clock. He paced around the living room, sometimes walking into the kitchen and then back out. He had been doing this for half an hour.

"Just a few more minutes, Diego. We'll get cooking in just a bit," his grandmother said with a warm smile while she rocked on her rocking chair. Her hands were busy crocheting a colorful sweater.

Diego dropped to the floor with a thump. He whined about wanting to start cooking now. His grandmother smiled as she listened to him complain, which eventually turned into him telling stories.

"Joshua Wong said that he's going to bring a type of noodle that's famous in China. He's also going to teach us how to use chopsticks," Diego said, sticking out his tongue as he concentrated on trying to use his pretend chopsticks.

"Oh?" his grandmother said, amused.

"Yeah! And Raj is bringing something called Chapati. He says it's a flat bread made from flour that's cooked on a pan. Grandma, did you know people in India sometimes eat with their hands?"

"Yes, I did," his grandmother said. "I've had friends from India, and I've tried it myself. The flavors are delicious. So, what are you going to bring for Multicultural Week, Diego?"

He thought for a moment. There were so many things he wanted to bring, but each student was only allowed one dish. Finally, he made up his mind.

"How about salsa? It's easy to make and I could bring chips! We've got chips don't we grandma?" he asked with bright, hopeful eyes.

"Yes, dear, we do. I picked up some white corn chips at the store earlier. Why don't you go get the salsa ingredients out?"

Diego was ecstatic. He rushed to the kitchen and carefully got the ingredients out of the fridge. For a nine-year-old, Diego was surprisingly interested in cooking and knew exactly what to do, thanks to his grandmother, who had taught him ever since he was little.

Diego got out fresh tomatoes, onions, jalapeño peppers, cilantro, garlic, and lime. Since he wasn't allowed to use grown-up knives, he waited for his grandmother to bring his special kid-safe kitchen tools.

A few minutes later, his grandmother joined him, and they started chopping, dicing, and cooking the ingredients together. It was a fun time. They talked about their day and almost forgot the salsa on the stove, but they laughed about it.

The next morning, they took the salsa out of the fridge and heated it up before Diego brought it to school. He was so excited and kept telling his friends about the dish.

"It's usually spicy but grandma and I made sure to make it mild today since I didn't bring drinks," he informed his friends.

Everyone couldn't wait to taste the different dishes on the table. The bowls and plates were still covered, but the delicious smells made their mouths water.

"Alright, kids! Let's open up our dishes, shall we?" Miss Valerie called out cheerfully with a clap.

The kids rushed to the table, pulling the lids off their containers. The room filled with amazing smells, and everyone got even more excited.

"Mm...it smells delicious! Can we start tasting the dishes now, Miss?" Mary asked. The kids around her nodded ferociously.

Miss Valerie chuckled and said, "Hold on there. Let's get you guys to introduce your dishes. How about we start with–" she paused and scanned the eager little faces and decided, "–Diego?"

"Yes, Miss!" Diego said, pulling his salsa closer. "My dish is called salsa. It's made from tomatoes—"

"Ew! I hate tomatoes," Suzie interrupted. Diego was surprised but continued.

"It also has lime, onion—"

"That sounds horrible!" Joshua said while pinching his nose.

"I'm not eating that," Gemma looked at the salsa strangely. "It's too red."

"Well, you're supposed to eat it with chips. I brought some," Diego said, but before he could pull out the chips, the kids started protesting.

Miss Valerie had to calm everyone down and told them not to be mean. But the damage was done. Diego felt terrible and embarrassed that everyone was making fun of how his salsa smelled and looked.

A few kids were curious and wanted to try it, but after hearing the teasing, they decided to eat other food instead. By the end of the day, Diego's salsa was completely untouched except for a few bites he ate himself.

When Diego got home, he was really upset. His grandmother noticed and asked, "What's wrong, Diego?"

Diego, who had been holding back his feelings, burst into tears. "Abuela, it was awful! The kids made fun of my salsa, and no one ate it!" he cried as his grandmother hugged him. She frowned.

"Don't worry about what they said, okay? Kids can be mean sometimes," she said, trying to comfort him. Eventually, Diego started to calm down.

"I don't understand. They didn't even try it yet. Why would they make fun of it?" Diego said while blowing his nose into a tissue.

"Sometimes people need time to accept something new. They aren't used to it yet, but maybe one day they'll start liking it," his grandmother explained.

Diego had an idea. He didn't want his classmates to miss out on how delicious Mexican food could be. So, he and his grandmother made a plan.

The next Saturday, they woke up early and went to the store to buy lots of ingredients.

When they got back, his grandmother started calling the parents of Diego's classmates and invited them over for Sunday afternoon.

Plenty of kids could make it, so Diego got to work, looking through cookbooks and watching video tutorials. He had special dishes in mind and wanted to make them himself.

Sunday afternoon arrived, and one by one, Diego's classmates arrived at his grandmother's house. They loved how cozy it felt and the smell of fresh roses in the air.

"Your grandma has a lovely home, Diego," Suzie said while hugging a fluffy pillow Diego's grandmother made.

"Is this your cat? He's so cute! What's his name?" Joshua asked while petting a snow-white cat that purred happily.

"His name is Gato, but he's not the reason I invited you all here today," Diego said with a grin. "Follow me to the sink, everyone!"

Eight kids followed Diego through an archway into the sparkling clean kitchen. The countertops and floors shined. Diego told everyone to wash their hands and grab a plate.

They did as they were told, looking both excited and a little confused. Diego began giving instructions.

"You'll see some corn husks on the plate. Take one, like I'm doing, and put it in front of you," he demonstrated. The kids followed along. "Now, take some of the dough that my grandma and I made and put it at the top of the corn husk."

Next, the kids chose their fillings, which included shredded chicken, fish, beans, and even mozzarella cheese. The last step was to fold the corn husks, and they were done! After folding two tamales each, they handed them to Diego's grandmother, who was ready to steam them.

The kids were still a little confused, but they were having so much fun that no one minded. The kitchen was filled with laughter and joy as they followed Diego's instructions.

When everything was done, Diego's grandmother gathered them in the dining room and, with a big smile, served the steamed tamales they had made along with a green dipping sauce.

The kids were excited to see their creations and started eating right away. From the first bite to the last, they couldn't stop praising how delicious the food was.

"Oh, I wish we had made more!" Suzie said.

"Yeah! This is delicious, Diego. Thank you," Joshua said with a mouth full of food.

"I'm glad you like them. The first dish we made is called tamales, and the second one is guacamole. They're both traditional Mexican foods," Diego explained.

The room went silent. Everyone looked at each other with wide eyes, still chewing.

"I'm sorry, Diego. I didn't know Mexican food would taste this good," Gemma said, lowering her head.

"Yeah, I'm sorry too. I thought it looked different from what I usually eat, so I was worried it wouldn't taste good," Suzie added.

Eventually, everyone started apologizing. It brought a big smile to Diego's face and an even wider one to his grandmother's. It felt great to know that once the children tried the food, they loved it!

For the rest of the time, the kids asked all sorts of questions about Mexican food and its history, and Diego and his grandmother were happy to answer.

From that day on, Diego and his friends made one rule: *Never turn down anything before trying it, because you might end up liking it.*

Diego was happy he shared his culture with his friends. He realized there was nothing to be ashamed of and that sometimes people make fun of things that are different. And that was okay! If he was proud of his heritage, no one could make him feel bad about it.

Diego's story shows us the value of being open-minded and the importance of sharing and celebrating our cultures. At first, his classmates judged his salsa without even trying it, but when Diego gave them another chance to taste his food, they realized how much they loved it. This teaches us that we shouldn't reject something just because it's different or unfamiliar. By embracing diversity, we can discover new things to enjoy and appreciate. Diego also learned that being proud of his heritage is important, and that true friends will support and respect what makes him unique.

The Lonely Bully

On Saturday, William brought a ball over to his dad and asked, "Hey dad, want to play catch?"

His dad barely looked at him as he walked by and said, "Not right now, buddy. I just got home from work."

William was disappointed, but he knew his dad was tired. He had been working extra hours, even on weekends. William hung his head and waited to watch a movie with his dad, but his dad never came out of his room.

He must have fallen asleep after his shower, William thought as he turned off the TV and went to bed.

The next weekend, William was with his mom. He waited eagerly for her to come home from work. Like his dad, his mom was also working harder than before. She had two jobs, and both were difficult and took up a lot of time.

As she stepped through the front door after work, William excitedly called, "Hi, mom! I made you some dinner." He brought her a bowl of salad, some scrambled eggs, and a big cup of her favorite green tea. It wasn't normally what people had for dinner, but it was all William knew how to make. He was only eleven, after all, and he wanted to show his mom how much he loved her.

William's mother looked at him with tired eyes. She didn't look too excited, only sending a small smile his way. She didn't mean to look unhappy- she was just exhausted. She patted his head and said, "Thank you, honey, but please try not to use up all the ingredients, alright? They're expensive."

She didn't mention how tight her budget had gotten ever since she and William's father got a divorce. But William understood that both his parents had been struggling lately.

"Okay, mom," William said softly.

Without another word, William's mother went to her room and accidentally dozed off, leaving poor William to eat the food he made for her.

Living with divorced parents wasn't easy. At first, it felt like a vacation, spending one week with his dad and the next with his mom. But after a year of doing this, William realized this was his new life. It felt like a vacation, and he always had a bag packed. He thought it was only temporary at first, but after a year of doing it, he realized that this was how his life was going to be from now on.

Over time, he started wondering where his actual home was. For a year now, his mother stayed in one house while his father stayed in another house. They weren't too friendly with each other anymore. They never greeted each other when dropping him off or picking him up. They just stayed in the car. He didn't understand what had happened between them or why things were different now.

He realized that none of his friends had this sort of living arrangement. They still lived in the same house, under one roof, with both their parents. When he went over to Evelyn's house the other day, her parents seemed so happy together! It started to feel like he didn't belong to either of his parents' homes.

At school, his grades started slipping, although, of course, his parents didn't notice. He was usually a bright student, but now he was getting average—or even below average—grades. He missed the days when his parents would care about his grades and push him to study.

One day, when Mr. Turner was returning their science tests, William got upset at his bad grade. Suddenly, he noticed that a boy in his class named Jay looked upset too. When he peaked over his shoulder, he saw that Jay had failed the science test.

"Hey, did you fail, Jay? William shouted, loud enough for the rest of the class to hear. Jay looked shocked and immediately pulled the hood of his sweater over his head as the other kids started whispering about him.

Instantly, William felt a lot better about his grade. *At least my grade isn't as bad as Jay's*, he thought to himself with a chuckle. He didn't think about how his words had hurt Jay. He only cared about making himself feel better.

During lunch the next day, William wanted to ask about the science homework that was due for the next lesson. He didn't finish the assignment, and the last thing he wanted to do was to copy someone else's homework. He knew copying was wrong. His mom had told him that if he didn't understand the homework, he should ask a friend or teacher for help instead of cheating.

"If you don't know how to do the assignment, you can ask your friends or teachers to help. But never copy the answers, William. If you do, you won't learn anything. You'll just end up cheating yourself out of a good education.

William put the advice out of his head. He called out to his friend Poppy but she didn't hear him over the hustle and bustle in the cafeteria. She kept walking while talking to her friend, Evelyn.

William knew that Poppy wasn't ignoring him on purpose but he got upset anyway. He remembered the times at home when his parents wouldn't give him the attention he wanted because of how tired they were. He didn't want to be ignored at school too. Angry, he stomped over to Poppy.

Stomp, stomp, stomp!

When he got close enough, he called her name again. This time, Poppy turned around with a big smile.

"Hi, William—" she started to say, but William yanked her hair.

"Ouch!" Poppy cried. William frowned at her.

"That's for not answering me when I called you the first time," he said in a frightening tone. He towered over Poppy, making her look like a tiny mouse next to him.

"I turned around as soon as I heard you, William!" Poppy said angrily, tears in her eyes as she rubbed the spot where he pulled her hair.

"Don't look at me like that!" William suddenly shouted.

Everyone in the cafeteria froze. They were surprised. His classmates had noticed that William had been changing lately, and not for the better. He had grown meaner and started showing less and less kindness towards his friends and classmates.

After that day, everyone was scared of William. No one wanted to play with him during recess, sit next to him in class, or join him at lunch. Even on the bus ride home, kids left the seat next to him empty. And when someone did sit beside him, William would tease or pinch them until they cried.

William was happy with his newfound power. He liked the feeling of being the most powerful kid in class. The only issue was that he became an outcast and started feeling lonely. But he'd finally found a way to release the frustration he felt from the problems he faced at home. He didn't feel good about being a bully, but he felt better overall. He felt strong and powerful, feelings he never felt at home.

One day while everyone was doing some silent reading in the classroom, Mr. Turner came in with a big smile on his face. "Class, eyes on me, please," he called, and all of the kids looked over at him with big, curious eyes.

"Today we have a new friend. Would you like to introduce yourself?" Mr. Turner asked, patting the boy on the back.

The boy's bright smile lit up the entire classroom. He nodded and said, "Hi everyone, I'm Acacius. It's nice to meet all of you--"

"What kind of silly name is that? It sounds like an octopus name!" William burst into laughter. Some kids shook their heads, while others felt bad for the new boy. It was his first day, and William was already giving him a hard time.

"William, that's not nice!" Mr. Turner said sternly.

Acacius simply smiled and explained, "Oh, that's alright. You probably haven't heard it before because it's Greek. I love the meaning behind my name—it means innocent. My father is Greek and my mother is American, so I'm a mix of the two."

William was surprised. Acacius wasn't scared or angry. He just explained calmly with a smile. His positive attitude was contagious, and soon everyone wanted to be friends with him.

During lunch, William decided to pick on Acacius again.

"Hey, worm head!" William called. Acacius turned and laughed. Everyone around him was surprised, but William was the most shocked.

"Oh, you must be talking about my hair. It's curly like my dad's, but I have my mom's blue eyes," he said again with a smile. William couldn't understand why Acacius wasn't afraid of him.

"Aren't you mad that I called you worm head?" William asked, his face turning red like a tomato.

Acacius shook his head. "No, my parents always taught me to be nice to everyone, even to people who are mean. Because we don't know what might be going on in their lives," he said. William froze.

After that, more kids felt brave enough to stand up to William when he was being mean. Acacius had inspired them.

William started thinking about what Acacius had said. It was true—no one knew what was going on at home for him, and he didn't really know what was truly happening in his friend's lives at home.

He thought about all of the terrible things he did to his friends and began to feel really guilty. Slowly, William decided to change his ways. Acacius became his role model. William admired how kind and gentle Acacius was and wanted to be more like him.

One morning, William got to school early and looked for the first two people he had hurt. From a distance, he saw Jay and Poppy talking by the lockers. He walked over quickly.

"Jay? Poppy?" he called nervously.

Jay thought that William was coming over to bully him again and grumbled, "What?"

William gulped.

"I just wanted to say I'm really sorry for teasing you when you failed that test, Jay. And I'm sorry for pulling your hair and yelling at you, Poppy. I know I was wrong, and I'll change," he said. He stared at their shoes and fumbled with his fingers, feeling nervous.

Jay and Poppy were shocked, but when they saw that William was serious, they smiled and said they would forgive him under one condition. They made him promise that he would never bully them again.

And he didn't. William went on to apologize to everyone he had hurt, but he knew that he had to prove that he had changed. So he worked on becoming a much kinder person. William's change of attitude earned him back all the friends he had lost. Over time, he and Acacius even became best friends.

At home, William decided to open up to his parents and tell them how he felt. They felt really bad for how they had been acting and promised to be there for him more.

William realized he had learned the wrong lesson before. Instead of bullying others to feel better and stronger, he should show kindness to build real friendships and support.

William's story teaches us that acting out of frustration and hurting others doesn't solve our problems—it only makes things worse. At first, William thought that being mean made him feel powerful, but he soon realized that it only left him feeling more alone. Through his new friend Acacius, he learned that true strength comes from kindness and understanding. By apologizing to those he hurt and changing his behavior, William found real friendships and the support he needed. This story reminds us that being kind is always the better choice, even when we're going through tough times.

The Shelter Helpers

"And remember, kids. These activities will count towards your mandatory volunteer hours," Mr. Hendrick said while reading the list of names on the paper. His eyes stopped on one name in particular and he looked up at the bright faces of his students.

"Matteo, you're volunteering at the homeless shelter again this week?" Mr. Hendrick asked with a smile.

Matteo nodded. "Yes, sir, with Emily and Ed," he said.

"You've volunteered there five weekends in a row now. You must really love helping at the shelter," Mr. Hendrick said.

It wasn't that Matteo loved it. He just found it was the easiest way to get his volunteer hours done. All Matteo had to do was toss a few ingredients into a big pot and serve it to the homeless. It was usually in the shade, so he didn't have to worry about sweating too much. At the end of every session, the leftover stew would be packed and sent home with the volunteers, which meant Matteo also got a free meal every weekend.

Matteo's mother suggested helping out at an animal shelter, but Matteo was terrified of dogs. His father suggested mentoring, but school was tough enough and Matteo didn't want to spend more time surrounded by books.

On the ride to the homeless shelter, Matteo sat in the backseat with his friends Emily and Ed. They whispered about school, tests, and how they didn't really like volunteering at the shelter.

"It's not the volunteering part that I don't like. It's that we have to help criminals and lazy people," Matteo said loudly enough for everyone in the car to hear. He crossed his arms, annoyed.

"Matteo! We do *not* talk about the homeless that way!" Emily's dad called in surprise and disappointment. "Actually, we don't talk about anyone that way."

"Why not? That's what an old man said last weekend," Emily added, trying to support her friend.

"Which old man?" her dad asked. He kept his eyes on the road but glanced at the kids in the rearview mirror with sad eyes.

"We don't know. He just passed by while we were serving food," Ed said.

"Well, sometimes adults can be wrong. That man was very wrong to say that about those poor homeless people," Emily's dad said firmly, leaving no room for the kids to talk back. "Some people just have it rough in life. That could be any one of us if we're not lucky."

The three children giggled in the back, finding it funny that Emily's father thought they might become homeless one day. Emily's dad sighed and drove the rest of the way in silence.

When they arrived at the shelter, Emily's dad got out of the car and followed the kids inside. They were confused because he usually didn't come with them. They gave him questioning looks, but he just smiled at them and disappeared around the corner.

An hour flew by as Matteo and his friends carelessly threw ingredients into the pot to make some stew. They knew the routine by now and could almost do it with their eyes closed. Then, they served the food and drinks to a long line of homeless people. The adults in charge advised volunteers to serve generous portions.

Just as they were finishing up, Emily's dad called the three of them over. He was standing with some of the homeless people who were clinging on to hot bowls of stew and cold juice boxes.

"Kids, meet my lovely new friends: Pam, Roger, and Janice. They've kindly agreed to share their stories and experiences with us," Emily's dad said. Then he gestured to the three unhappy kids, "And these three are Emily, Matteo, and Ed."

Pam was an old woman. Her hair had turned completely gray and she was hunched over. In her trembling hand was a wooden cane that she used as a walking stick. She had almost no teeth left and her face was mostly wrinkled. But her smile was bright and beautiful.

Roger looked a bit younger, maybe around Matteo's father's age. He had a thick beard and tired, sunken eyes. His clothes were torn in places and his teeth were rotting. He had a long scar on his arm that looked painful. He smiled at the kids but it didn't quite reach his eyes.

Lastly, Janice looked a lot younger. She might have been fresh out of high school. She had a frightened look in her eyes that didn't seem to ever go away. Her long, brown hair was tangled and messy. When the kids looked closer, they saw her hair was also stiff and greasy. She was extremely thin and pale as a ghost.

"Lovely to meet you kids," Pam smiled. The kids gave her shy smiles in return.

"Come closer, kids, and I'll tell you how I became homeless," Pam said. They all gathered around as she started her story. "Just a few years ago, I lived in a big house with my daughter Avery, her husband, and my two little grandchildren. My life was perfect except for some small arguments with my daughter," she said with a sad smile.

"Then one night, on my birthday, Avery told me her husband didn't like me living with them anymore. They had thought I was only staying for a little while. No one had told me this," Pam explained, her eyes filling with tears. "They eventually kicked me out of the house, and with nowhere to go, I ended up living on the streets."

Emily and Ed gasped, but Matteo was confused and upset. He had lost his grandparents years ago and missed them a lot. He couldn't imagine treating his parents like that – he loved them so much.

Then Roger shared his story. He had worked really hard to start his own business, but a flood ruined everything. After that, it became impossible to rebuild the business. He started falling behind on his bills and rent.

"My family and friends loaned me some money a few times, but they couldn't do it forever. Things got worse, and soon I was thrown out of my home without a dime to my name and forced to live in the streets."

Matteo felt shocked. There were so many questions in his head, but he pushed them aside for now.

Janice's story was also sad. She had been sent to juvenile prison for stealing, but no one knew the truth. "I stole food from a store to feed my little brother and sister," she explained. "Our parents died in a car crash when I was seventeen, and our aunt, who was supposed to take care of us, didn't want us around. She was a drug addict and rarely fed us."

"But they don't know that what I stole was food from the store to feed my little brother and sister. Both my parents died in a car crash when I was seventeen and our aunt was supposed to look after us, but she didn't want us around. She was a drug addict and rarely had food for us."

She went on to explain how she wasn't allowed back into her aunt's house because her aunt saw her as a thief, and so she was forced onto the streets.

"It's sad because I used to be an excellent student when I was in school. My dream was to become a doctor, but there's no chance of that happening right now," Janice said.

Matteo thought for a moment and then asked, "Why don't you just get jobs? Wouldn't that help?"

Janice sighed. "It's really hard to get a job when you've been to jail. People don't listen to your story. Once they see a criminal record, they won't hire you."

"No one wants to hire a woman my age, dear. We just have to find ways to get by," Pam said in her crackly old voice.

Pam explained that most of the time, "getting by" meant trying to sell or exchange something for food or begging for spare change.

Then Roger added, "Besides, when you go in for a job interview you need clean work clothes, a permanent address, a phone number... it's difficult for us to have those things. Even basic jobs think twice about hiring homeless people. So we try to work in any way we can to get the money."

The kids listened to some other stories as well about how difficult it was to get medicine, how they were always hungry, not knowing when the next meal was going to come, and shivering while sleeping on the cold hard ground at night.

Emily was crying after hearing their stories, while Ed and Matteo were sniffling. Matteo couldn't believe just how cruel the world could be.

The ride home was quiet while everyone thought about the stories they had just heard. Emily's dad finally broke the silence.

"So Matteo, do you still think that the homeless are just lazy criminals?" he asked.

Matteo hung his head in shame, regretting ever saying such an awful thing. "No, they've been through so much, and we should help them as much as we can," he replied.

That day, Matteo decided he wanted to volunteer more, not just to finish his hours, but to help people. Emily and Ed were also eager to make a change, even if it was a small one.

Back at school, Matteo spoke to his teacher about wanting to create more awareness homelessness, and Mr. Hendrick was more than happy to help. Mr. Hendrick decided that the following weekend, the entire class would take a trip to the homeless shelter to volunteer.

Other teachers also began talking about homelessness and why people might end up without a home. They discussed what the kids in their classes could do to help.

On Friday, the day before the class trip to the homeless shelter, Mr. Hendrick called on Matteo to share his experiences while volunteering and asked what jobs the kids would be expected to do at the shelter, and if they could bring anything to donate.

They created a list of items people could donate. Many blankets, jackets, coats, shoes, socks, and other clothes were donated. Some parents even donated money. Lucy's father, who was a wealthy business owner, arranged for food and hygiene products to be donated as well.

Matteo felt truly thankful for all the blessings in his life—plenty of food, a warm home, and a caring family. Talking to the homeless people at the shelter made him realize they were doing their best with the tough situations they were facing. They deserved to be treated with kindness, not judgment. He felt compassion for those less fortunate and knew he wanted to help in any way he could.

Matteo's story teaches us not to judge others based on appearances or assumptions. At first, he thought the homeless were lazy or didn't want to help themselves, but after hearing their stories, he realized that many people face challenges that are hard to imagine. Matteo learned the importance of kindness, compassion, and helping those in need. This story reminds us that everyone deserves to be treated with respect and understanding, and that even small acts of kindness can make a big difference.

The Unkind Leader

"Alright then, so we all agree that Kai should be team captain?" Miss Amelia, the debate teacher, asked.

Everyone nodded happily. Kai was the best debater on the team, and his teammates thought it made sense for him to be captain.

"This is going to be so much fun, Kai!" Evelyn clapped happily. Their other teammates, Jason, Missy, and Howard, agreed. Everyone was giggling and talking amongst themselves.

Kai felt that he was suited to be captain, too. For the past eleven years, his mother always said that he walked around with a book in his hand—even before he could read. Kai read so much that he was certain he knew nearly everything there was to know.

As his teammates discussed how fun it was going to be to practice together, Kai frowned. He snorted and said, "Debate isn't supposed to be *fun*. It's serious business and we need to practice really hard if we're going to win."

"Oh, of course, we'll practice hard, Kai," Missy said, looking confused. "But we can still have fun too, can't we?"

Kai crossed his arms. "No, I don't think it should be fun at all. I'm team captain now and I say we practice seriously. No more giggling, laughing, and fooling around," Kai announced sternly.

His friends were surprised by Kai's attitude. Normally, he was fun and easygoing, but today, he seemed strict. They didn't argue with him, thinking maybe he was just having a bad day.

Practice went on, but was dull without the usual laughter and fun. The team worked hard, but something was missing. After practice, Kai rushed home, eager to share the news with his parents.

"Mom! Dad!" he called as he burst through the front door.

His parents peeked their heads out from the living room. "What is it, honey?" his mom asked.

"I'm the new debate team captain! Can you believe it?" He cheered and went on to tell his parents about the voting and how he created a new rule about practice being more serious. He stood proudly and his parents looked at each other before smiling down at Kai.

"That's wonderful, sweetie!" his mom said, giving him a big hug. "We're so proud of you."

"Great work, buddy!" his dad added with a grin. "Just make sure you don't let all that power go to your head. Being a good captain means being kind and helping your team."

Kai didn't really understand what his dad meant but nodded anyway. He was just excited to be the leader.

The next day, practice came again, but it wasn't as fun as usual because of Kai's new rule. Miss Amelia noticed how boring it was and tried to get the kids to talk about fun things. But Kai stopped it right away.

"No, Miss," he said. "We can't play around if we want to win."

Miss Amelia frowned. "You can still win while having fun, Kai. Fun doesn't equal to failure," she tried to tell him, but Kai didn't change his mind. So, practice continued the way Kai wanted it.

The regional debate finals were just around the corner and the team decided to have a quick session to discuss potential topics they should focus on.

"I saw an interesting one about whether or not school uniforms should be banned," Howard suggested.

"No, it's not going to be something as simple as that," Kai objected.

Jason spoke up next. "How about if mobile phones should be allowed in classrooms?"

Kai shook his head again.

"Okay, what about the pros and cons of social media for students?" Evelyn asked.

Again, Kai turned the idea down with a big frown on his face. He felt like the topics were too simple and not worth practicing. So the team went on listing off what seemed like perfectly good topics, yet none were good enough for Kai. He simply shook his head and rejected each and every one.

"It's like you guys aren't even trying. Can't you think of anything a bit more difficult? I don't want to practice on baby topics," Kai rudely said as he crossed his arms over his chest.

Jason was starting to get tired of Kai's behavior. He stood up and slammed his hands on the table once Miss Amelia left the room.

"I don't know what's gotten into you, Kai, but you need to stop acting so bossy," Jason said, his face red with anger.

Kai was surprised by Jason's outburst, but he didn't want to back down. "I'm the captain, like it or not. So you have to listen to me, and I said to think of harder topics to practice."

"Why don't you come up with some, then?" Missy asked, also annoyed but trying to stay calm. "We've been giving all the ideas, and you just keep saying no. So why don't you help us?"

"*I* don't have to suggest anything because *I'm* the captain," Kai said again. Kai said loudly. He walked up to the board and started writing everyone's names in columns. When he finished, he turned to face them. "Since I'm the captain, you have to listen to me."

"I'm giving everyone in this room one day to come up with creative topics that we can practice. Otherwise, I'll be forced to kick you off the team," Kai said. He was trying to appear stern and strict, like their principal who wore his glasses at the tip of his nose. But his friends weren't scared at all. They just felt upset with how Kai was acting and didn't want to be around him anymore.

No one spoke. Jason grabbed his bag and stormed out of the room. Soon, everyone else followed.

Kai was really mad. He called for them to come back, but they ignored him. Right before leaving, Evelyn turned and said, "We picked you as captain, but you're treating us really badly. Friends don't do that."

Kai stared at her through his thick-rimmed glasses. He huffed and said, "In here, I'm not your friend. I'm your captain, and you have to do what the captain says if you want to win."

Evelyn tried to reason with Kai, but he wouldn't listen. So, she walked out too. Kai was about to shout about telling Miss Amelia that everyone skipped practice, but before he could, the teacher came back in. She had overheard the conversation and asked Kai to sit down. Kai sat, ready to complain about the whole team. But Miss Amelia spoke first.

"Kai, do you like being the captain?" she asked. Kai nodded excitedly.

"The only thing I don't like is that my teammates are stubborn. They don't listen to me. I'm just trying to get them in the right mindset," Kai said, letting out a sigh.

"And what mindset is that?" Miss Amelia asked, raising an eyebrow.

Kai sat up straight, feeling confident. "A winner's mindset! I can't have them goofing around or practicing on easy topics. Anyone can do that! If we want to win, we have to be different," he said proudly.

Miss Amelia nodded, thinking about what he said. "But wouldn't it be better to practice something, anything, together? Look at today. You argued with the team, and now no one practiced at all."

Kai knew what Miss Amelia meant, but he still thought his way was right.

The next day, the team met again, but things felt tense. No one was talking to Kai. They ignored him and chatted among themselves. Kai got frustrated and went to Miss Amelia to complain. The teacher came over and asked the group to start practicing a topic.

Immediately, they picked a topic one of them had suggested the day before and excluded Kai from the practice session. Kai got mad again and shouted that he was the captain and they had to listen to him. The team continued to ignore him, kept happening every day until the day of the competition. Kai practiced alone, refusing to join the others.

On the day of the competition, Miss Amelia was worried. The team wasn't working together at all. They practiced separately, and it was clear their teamwork was falling apart.

"Don't worry, Miss. I'll win this, with or without them," Kai said confidently.

Miss Amelia frowned. "This is a team effort, Kai. You can't win alone," she said. She was disappointed that Kai still didn't understand the importance of teamwork.

The competition began with a screech over the loudspeaker followed by an announcement.

"Next up, Lake West Elementary versus Willowbrook Elementary. Debaters take your positions," the chairperson announced.

"Willowbrook, you're taking the negative side," the chairperson told Kai, Evelyn, and Jason, while Missy and Howard stood on the side as reserves.

"Okay, so we're arguing against the topic. Got it?" Kai said in a mocking tone.

"We know how this works, Kai," Jason whispered, annoyed. "We're on the debate team too." Evelyn ignored them as she set up her notebook.

"Your topic is... the ban of school uniforms. Lake West will argue for the ban, and Willowbrook will argue against it," the chairperson reminded them.

Evelyn glared at Kai. This was the exact topic Howard had suggested during practice, but Kai had said it was too easy.

As the other team spoke, Kai, Evelyn, and Jason wrote down their notes. But they didn't talk about who would say what. Kai stubbornly waited for his turn to speak. He didn't want to help his teammates since they didn't listen to him.

"Willowbrook Elementary, first speaker," the chairperson spoke.

Kai stood up, adjusted the microphone, and made his point that school uniforms shouldn't be banned because they create unity and equality.

Jason, the second speaker, started to panic. His point was the same as Kai's, and now he had nothing to say. He tried to think of something new, but his mind went blank.

Evelyn realized Jason was panicking but couldn't help him, as he had already stood up and walked to the podium.

Jason's entire body shook with fear and sweat dripped down his face. He brought his mouth to the microphone and he still had no idea what to say. The only thing he muttered was, "Uh..." before sitting back down, completely stuck.

Willowbrook lost the debate, and the ride back to school was filled with arguing.

"It's Jason's fault! He froze and didn't say anything!" Kai yelled.

"No! It's Kai's fault for not letting us practice at all," Evelyn shouted.

Missy jumped into the conversation. "It's all your faults for not working together. You're all selfish and childish!" she cried.

The fighting immediately stopped. Everyone went quiet. They all started thinking about their part in the loss. Kai knew it was mostly his fault. He had been so bossy and power hungry that he had completely ignored what was most important: valuing and respecting his friends' ideas.

"I'm sorry," Kai suddenly said. Everyone looked at him. "I'm sorry for not listening and for misusing my power. I was just really excited."

The team wasn't sure if they should forgive him after how he had acted. Miss Amelia stepped in.

"I think you can trust Kai to change," she said. Then she turned to him, "You need to learn to be a better captain, Kai."

Kai looked up at her, "How can I do that?"

Miss Amelia smiled. "Start by listening to everyone's ideas. A good leader is a good listener. You also need to explain why you're making decisions. Also, a good captain needs think about what's best for the team."

The next day, the team practiced for the next competition. Kai followed Miss Amelia's advice. He listened to his teammates and worked together with them. His friends started to trust him again. They were happy to have Kai as their captain, now that he was working with them and not bossing them around.

Kai learned an important lesson: a good leader builds up their team, while a bad one tears it apart. From that moment on, he vowed to always be the kind of leader who listens, supports, and helps his team succeed.

> *Kai's story teaches us that leadership isn't just about being in charge; it's about listening to others and working together as a team. At first, Kai thought that being strict and controlling would help his team win, but he soon realized that without listening to his teammates, they couldn't succeed. By learning to respect their ideas and collaborate, Kai became a better leader, and his team started to trust him again. This shows that real leadership is about bringing people together, supporting them, and making sure everyone feels valued.*

The Video Game Glitch

Henry Nguyen was a really good gamer for someone who was only twelve. He started playing video games with his older sister, Leah, when he was eight years old.

His parents didn't mind him playing games because Henry was great at managing his time. He always did well in school, helped out around the house, and got all his chores done. He was kind to everyone too.

However, Henry often tried to take shortcuts instead of doing things the proper way.

For example, when he had math homework, he used a calculator to finish quickly. But because he didn't show his work, the teacher gave him a warning and took away some points from his grade.

Another time, his dad found him wearing two pairs of jeans—one over the other! Henry wobbled around like a panda and could barely eat, but he claimed it was faster than wasting time changing out of his outside clothes once they got home.

Henry was a nice kid but often did silly things. His parents, friends, and teachers were used to it.

One day, while Henry was playing Fortnite—his favorite video game—he realized he was doing much better than his teammates. After the game, other players praised him and suggested he should try to play in tournaments.

Henry hadn't thought about that before, but it sounded like a good idea. So, he practiced as much as he could and watched videos of top players to learn new tricks.

His parents were very supportive of him.

"I know you're an incredible player, and it would be great for you to play with other top gamers. But don't forget to have fun—after all, it's just a game," his mother would often remind him.

"Alright, mom, I'll remember that," Henry always said.

One day, Henry rushed downstairs, sweaty and excited. "Mom! Dad!" he shouted.

His parents hurried over, worried something was wrong. "What happened?" his dad asked.

"I qualified! I'm one of the finalists for the Fortnite tournament!" Henry cheered, hugging his parents.

They laughed in relief. "Congratulations, buddy!"

That night, his mom made Henry's favorite meal for dinner—burgers, curly fries, and his favorite chocolate drink, Yoo-hoo. . His sister, Leah, even got him some pizza on her way home from her part-time job. Things couldn't have been going any better for Henry.

A week later, all the tournament finalists met over a video call. Henry was excited to meet other gamers besides his sister. The other finalists were friendly and kind. They all got along so well that they promised each other that no matter who won, they would stay friends and play together after the tournament ended.

The tournament was still months away, and Henry spent all his free time practicing. But as the tournament got closer, he started feeling nervous. Everyone at school knew about it and was cheering him on.

"Good luck, Henry!" Peter shouted after school.

"Make sure you win!" Isaiah said with a big smile.

Even his neighbor congratulated him, saying it was exciting that he had made it so far.

But Henry started worrying—what if he didn't win? Would everyone be disappointed in him? Would they stop being friendly? Would they stop believing in him? He wasn't sure, but it made him feel stressed.

Soon, playing Fortnite didn't feel fun anymore. It felt like hard work. Practicing felt more like a job, and watching videos of pro players felt like a school assignment.

I can't wait for the tournament to be over, Henry thought as he buried his head in his hands.

He was stressed but didn't want to worry his parents or friends, so he always put on a happy face. He knew keeping secrets wasn't right, but he wasn't sure what else to do.

One day, while reading about Fortnite strategies, he stumbled upon something surprising—a cheat code. It was a shortcut that would give him an unfair advantage by keeping his health full no matter what. With the competition just a week away, Henry felt more confident, thinking there was no way he could lose now. He had a secret weapon.

On the day of the tournament, Henry arrived at the hall with his family cheering him on. He played comfortably, not trying too hard because he knew he couldn't lose with his secret trick. But as he kept winning, his opponents grew suspicious.

After winning every single game back-to-back, Henry was beaming with pride. He cheered for himself, feeling on top of the world. He rushed over to meet his new friends—who had been his opponents during the tournament—eager to celebrate with them.

"Did you see that? I won!" he said proudly.

His friends just frowned at him. Henry thought it was strange that they didn't congratulate him. They were usually very supportive and had made a promise to remain friends even after the tournament.

"What's wrong?" he asked.

At first, the group remained silent. Instead of cheering, his friends just frowned. Alice spoke up. "We know you cheated, Henry. There's no way your health didn't go down at all after getting hit so many times."

Henry's heart sank. He hadn't expected to get caught, and now he was filled with panic. What could he say? If he admitted to cheating, he'd be disqualified, and all his hard work would go to waste. Confused and ashamed, Henry slowly walked away from his friends, guilt washing over him.

He knew he couldn't keep it from his parents any longer.

"I have something to tell you," he said nervously when he found them. He bit his lip, trying to hold back his nerves. Despite his stuttering, he finally blurted out the whole story.

His parents and sister listened quietly. He could see the disappointment in their faces, and it made him feel even worse. He started to cry.

His mother pulled him into a hug. "Oh, sweetheart, I'm so sorry we didn't notice how stressed you were," she said softly.

"We were so caught up in the excitement of the tournament that we forgot to check if you were doing okay. We're sorry, buddy," his father added.

His sister Leah, who was also a gamer, understood how hard it was to admit when you did something wrong and face losing an achievement. But she knew Henry had to make things right.

After explaining why honesty and having fun while gaming were important, she said, "I think you know what you need to do, Henry." Leah smiled warmly at him.

Henry nodded and decided to fix the mess he had caused as well as try to mend his friendship. He headed straight to the judges' stand and explained nervously.

Henry nodded and decided to fix the mess he had caused. He headed straight to the judges' stand, feeling nervous but determined.

"Hi, I'm Henry. I won the Fortnite tournament, but I need to admit something." The judges listened carefully. Henry gulped and continued, "I used a cheat code to win."

The judges were shocked but had no choice—they disqualified him. Though it hurt to lose the champion title, Henry knew he had done the right thing.

"I'm really sorry for everything," he said. "You're right, I used a cheat code, and it wasn't fair. I'll never do it again."

"We appreciate the apology," Alice said sadly, "but you did take a spot one of us deserved."

Henry looked at her shyly and replied, "Actually, I told the judges I cheated. You're the real winner, Alice. I've been disqualified."

Alice was stunned. "Wow, I didn't expect that. Thank you, Henry!" She gave him a big hug.

Henry realized that cheating wasn't worth the trouble that followed, and it was much better to play a fair game and lose than to cheat and win.

Henry realized that cheating wasn't worth the trouble. It was far better to play fair and lose than to cheat and win. From that day on, Henry played games honestly and had more fun. He might have lost the tournament, but he won back the trust and respect of his friends—and for Henry, that was the biggest win of all.

> *Henry's story teaches us the importance of honesty and the consequences of taking shortcuts. While Henry was talented and passionate about gaming, he learned that cheating to win only led to guilt and disappointment. By admitting his mistake and making things right, Henry discovered that true success comes from playing fair and enjoying the journey, not just the end result. This story reminds us that strong character and respect from others are more valuable than any victory achieved through dishonesty.*

Conclusion

The ten boys we followed in this book each had their own struggles and challenges, but they also had the courage to learn from their mistakes. With the support of their families, friends, and teachers, they became stronger, kinder, and wiser. We all make mistakes—that's how we learn and grow.

Mistakes don't define you—they guide you. Every mistake is a chance to improve and become even better than you were before. Failure is just learning in disguise, and learning makes you stronger.

A bit of advice from me: you'll face challenges in life, but as long as you stay kind, brave, and thoughtful, there's nothing you can't overcome. And when times get tough, remember you don't have to do it alone. Turn to your trusted grown-ups or your close friends. They're always there for you.

You are an incredible person, doing the best you can every day. Always believe that!

Before we go, here's a special message just for you: You are smart, kind, brave, and full of talent. You're doing great things, and there's so much more ahead for you. Always remember how much you're loved and appreciated—so be sure to love yourself just as much! Keep learning, stay kind, and keep being you. See you soon!

14337958R00049